Praise for *Americorona*

Philip Kolin's **Americorona** captures the essence of the pandemic with heartfelt compassion and careful attention to medical, economic, and social details. His poems share in the tragedy as well as the victories of health care providers, their patients and their families. Kolin's poems reflect the fragility and struggles of the human condition during the pandemic by insightfully focusing on what we must do not only to survive but to conquer fear and uncertainty.

—Steven A. Gustafson, D.O., FCAP, FASP, CS
College of Osteopathic Medicine
William Carey University

Philip Kolin looks at the world through plague-colored lenses, but he starts with the Black Death that raged through 14th-century Europe and other historical pandemics to show how they relate to the COVID virus. And why not? Circumstances may change, but human nature doesn't. We always learn from adversity, always remember, as one of his poems says, "when the world was in love with faces." The poems in **Americorona** are smart, compassionate, and aware in a way that brings those qualities out in anyone who reads them.

—David Kirby
Robert O. Lawton Distinguished Professor of English
Florida State University

In *Americorona* Philip Kolin demonstrates he is both a disciple of history and a prophet regarding the COVID pandemic. His powerful collection touches upon almost every feeling we as Americans have had about COVID, including hope and salvation which Kolin deftly weaves in so many of these poems. Each of the seven sections into which the collection is divided begins with a poem about a relevant historical pandemic that Kolin brings to life with glowing detail. For instance, the section focusing on hunger and discrimination starts with a poem on the Irish Potato Famine where the virus "snuck away from Mexico and sucked the life out of the potato crop" or the section on long-haulers opens with a poem about a cholera ship where the dying crew spend their time working on "parafining chipped planks" and making sure they do not break away from the "iron waves" that imprison the ship in quarantine. I am ready to re-read *Americorona* and recommend it to anyone who has suffered because of the COVID pandemic, which, I think, is just about all of us.

—*Dominic Reisig*
Professor and Extension Specialist
Department of Entomology and Plant Pathology
North Carolina State University

"O that my head were a spring of water, and my eyes a fountain of tears, so that I might weep day and night for the slain of my poor people," so spoke Jeremiah (9:1) centuries ago. We hear the same pleas in Philip Kolin's new, amazing collection of poems on COVID-19. Kolin has found modern words to mourn the many and so much that America has lost because of the pandemic. These memory-holding poems speak for the children, for the separated families, for the desperate poor, for the health care professionals sheltering the sick, and for the dying and their families. But Kolin's poems also let us hear the masked and the non-masked alike, the naysayers who deny the very existence of the pandemic. Yes, these poems express grief but they also offer the healing balm of hope. Kolin's poems are important for anyone interested in the history of COVID. I strongly recommend this beautiful book.

—*Margaret Humphreys*, *M.D., Ph.D.*
Josiah Charles Trent Professor of History
Duke University

AMERICORONA

AMERICORONA

Poems about the Pandemic

Philip C. Kolin

RESOURCE *Publications* · Eugene, Oregon

AMERICORONA
Poems about the Pandemic

Resource Publications
An Imprint of Wipf and Stock Publishers
199 W. 8th Ave., Suite 3
Eugene, OR 97401

www.wipfandstock.com

PAPERBACK ISBN: 978-1-6667-3307-5
HARDCOVER ISBN: 978-1-6667-2736-4
EBOOK ISBN: 978-1-6667-2737-1

for Juliet

Table of Contents

Preface

There are three types of poems here. The majority focus on COVID-19 and the key issues it raised in American culture, economy, and health, from late 2019 through early 2021. Leading off each of the seven sections on COVID-19 are poems about historical pandemics that foreshadow, parallel, or highlight the tragic events of this most current pandemic. These historical poems provide context and direction for the collection as a whole. Interspersed among the COVID-19 and historical poems are experimental, poems on such subjects as the memories of breathing, the loss of sunshine, the effects of brain fog, and the "exhaustion of monotony" in the pandemic years, and beyond.

Acknowledgments

I am grateful to the following journals where earlier versions of these poems appeared:

"Polio Kids, Chicago, 1952." *After Hours* 34 (Winter 2017): 34.

"Cotton in the Time of the Corona Pandemic" *Valley Voices* 20:2 (Fall 2020): 36.

"*Nuestra Nueva Casa.*" Portside.org, posted September 25, 2020.

"Sheltering." *Blood and Thunder* [University of Oklahoma College of Medicine] (Fall 2020): 41.

"COVID *Abattoir.*" *New Verse News*, www.newversenews.com posted October 20, 2020.

"Screw COVID. I Went to Sturgis." *San Pedro River Review* 13.1 (Spring 2021): 54.

"Worship During the Pandemic." *Spiritus* 21.1 (Spring 2021): 159.

"Stark Distancing." *Paterson Literary Review* (2021): 124.

"COVID Brain Fog." *Paterson Literary Review* (2021): 126.

I: How It All Started

When the Black Death Crept into Our Town, 1349

Dunwich, England

We went to bed hearing about it. There'd been an outbreak
in the towns around us, though last night the air smelled clean.
But in the morning we found ugly black welts
under our armpits and groins, some the size of rotten apples,
all oozing pus. Then we heard screeching in the streets.

They say the wells were poisoned, and that evil spirits
had seeded the air with fleas to torment us. We dared not
touch each others' clothes for fear of being infected.
In the frenzied gloom that followed, some neighbors
strapped on masks drenched in garlic to save themselves.

Still, they died. The doctors insisted that the bodies
of the sick must have the black bile drilled out of
their skulls. It would work faster than a fistful
of leeches. But the priests proclaimed that because
we had sinned so grievously and so often God

commanded the planets to spin their punishing wrath
on us. As the number of dead increased every day,
and grave diggers became fewer and fewer,
we learned the pope, too, had gone silent.
Our feeble cries could not reach God's ear.

How the Corona Plague Began, November 2019

25 million voices worldwide
want to know how they were stricken
with this Corona plague.

Most never went into a bat cave,
used guano for fertilizer, ate
palm civet, picked parasites

off the scales of Malayan pangolins,
savored white owl and starlings,
or coveted wild blood-stained hog.

Yet we have a right to know
if any of these creatures incubated
this bat-borne virus that spilled

over into patient zero, the first
human being to begin the fatal cough
that spread around the globe.

Wuhan still remains the epicenter—
whether at its wet market or possibly
from the Institute of Virology that leaked

the death curse that threatened
to surpass earlier pandemics.
The trajectory always fatal, the source

still unknown. Not even the CIA
can say for certain how it started
or when it will ever end.

But the virus is not going away
in the early April breeze.

Corona Vignettes

Can a mother quarantine her unborn baby
from this virus. When he's born, how will
she hold him. Must he wear a mask made from
Q-tip cotton, and do his diapers have to be PPE grade.
His cough dare not spatter more than two feet.

School children now sprout strawberry tongues, their faces
white as paste, their foreheads concaved from endless
temperature checks. Forbidden to touch doorknobs, dinner
plates, keyboards, they need to be measured for zinc-

lined suits, making it easier to wipe off lingering
droplets. For anyone short of breath, the health dept.
will deliver rations of air six feet from their front door,
though these oxygen squads have a tough job getting
around the dead, stacked like wood to the curbs.

Nursing home residents lie behind glass
coffin windows. Their pantomime lips speak
without sound, their smiles empty hieroglyphs.
Only fingers can visit them.

Cotton in the Time of the Corona Pandemic

Like miniature atomic bombs, COVID's aerosols spiral,
stuff the air, burrow into bodies, lurk for hours, days,
weeks. Even cell phones are infected—three syllables expel

a barrage of fatal droplets. Faces have become
a battleground. Our mouths, eyes, noses
are the new Dunkirks, the new Hiroshimas.
Our hands have turned against us like enemy agents.

Still, cotton can save us. Homemade quilted cotton masks
thwart the virus. Quilting is the very fabric of our history.
Puritans, Quakers, African American Guilds—all quilters.

Last Good Friday the full moon, half hidden
by clouds, looked like it was wearing a cotton mask
as if heaven itself told us how to make sure this plague
could pass over us.

I Remember When Sunlight Fell on Faces

I remember when the world was in love with faces,
when sunlight fell fully across them as if anointed
with chrism, the air so soothing you couldn't breathe enough.

Remember when your face felt sunshine at picnics,
on the lake, at weddings, and how people strode down
crowded afternoon streets, every passer-by a shareholder
in this company of glorious encounters. Remember

when beaches were shrines of light, oil lustering faces,
our colorful quilted blankets unfolding next to others
like bungalows in a sunny Chicago neighborhood.

Singing, too, was better in the sunlight, notes furling farther,
sounds so much more mellow. Smiles served as passports
to friendship, community, love, memories.
Artists like Minjun painted themselves smiling.

When a gentle shower caressed us, we didn't worry
that it grimaced the world with toxic particles forcing us
to hide our smiles.

Dancing Before COVID-19 Struck

We used to dance on Fridays,
silver smooth, and on Saturdays,
salsa hot, women with staccato hearts
keeping time with our smiles.
They were trellises with spring
wildflowers in our arms even
in the middle of barren January.
Their eyes were palettes of fantasy.

They were compasses, too, steering us
toward desire with twinkles, rondes
sweet flirtations, promenade voyages.
Dates lasted two minutes; courtships
two hours. Photos snapped on polished,
mirrored dance floors celebrated
horoscopes with Venus rising.

But then COVID butt in and boarded up
the dance halls; our bodies went into mothballs
and we forgot what to do with them.

Stark Distancing

The world has shrunk to six feet
ironically the same grave distance
separating the quick from the dead.

We are living in a world of fevers—
our foreheads determine the degree
to which we can venture outside,
stay locked up at home, or end up in a hallway
outside a breathless ICU.

We are forging a new geography of touch
where kindness, expressions of love
are rationed—a laugh, a tear, a kiss, a hug, a pat
on the back—or outlawed. Brides have to stand
at least six feet from their grooms, each allowed
to blow only one virtual, shaky kiss.

Soon the government will ban passports
and instead issue permits to travel but no more
than 30 feet a day, including inside your own home.

Testing

To be or not to be tested
whether to let that puffy swab
like some stiff cigarette poke up
your nose in search of protein particles

or not. Tests cannot promise 100 percent accuracy.
You could be negative at 8 am but positive
at noon. You might feel fine but
already have infected your whole family.

A nagging cough might fret you off
to the doctor's for a test only to find out
you have allergies.

Or you could have aches and pain
and feel like a razor blade has cut
your throat and fear you have COVID.

But what if the test says you have the flu—
what a relief—or, worst case scenario,
you have the twinemic of flu and COVID.

But whatever your results, be ready
for multiple tests. Long haulers have had
dozens of them.

Lockdown

Our house is in a different country without ever moving away.
A storm of devices, microwaves, discs, cabinets, finches, and assorted
CDs has blown through each room making the house gain 500
pounds. It cries a lot now, and rooms frequently get into fights
with each other. More doors, they clamor. More windows. The
roof says the sky speaks a language it can no longer shelter. The
clouds have turned into concrete and the stars' lights are dimmed.
We can't go outside more than three times a week and then we
have to dress in PPE's. The kids, though, can go to school in their
pajamas. We dare not get within breathing
distance of our neighbors. Sometimes they holler at us, but we're
thinking of electrifying our fence. The workday has been amped
up from 8 hours to 14. Our employer says what else can you do
during a lockdown. So why not be productive? We've torn apart
the furniture to make room for an office, piano recitals, yoga,
mock executions, tax audits, replays of *Divorce Court*, survival
games, and reruns of horse operas. Every visitor from the
cleaning lady to the doctor comes through Zoom, whom, we fear,
are spying on us like that eye on the lopped off pyramid on a dol-
lar bill. *Lysol*'s the new liquid gold, traded on the dark web,
if you can figure how to sneak it into the house.

Divorce Corona Style

They may live in the same house,
but demand separate zip codes.

A couple Zooms each other
from one room to another.

Like their vows, they opt for anything disposable—
paper plates, cups, napkins, anniversaries.

They wear rubber gloves to reduce the danger
of touching each other's fingerprints.

They split health insurance costs—
her coverage extends from the waist up;

his from the waist down—
another way to asunder their vows.

When the day arrives for their FaceTime
divorce proceedings, they wear masks

and agree that any leftover
emotions should go to the therapists.

Worship During the Pandemic

Call ahead if you want one of the 75 sheltered seats
in this church that used to house 700 worshipers up
and down the nave, and along the side altars.
But the seats are not always vacant; angels occupy them,
sometimes more than 900 or more to a seat,
since they can kneel on a candle wick
or expand to hallowed stars in this pandemic gloom.

COVID demands we wear masks at church,
but think of them as vestments to keep sin
away. Or sacramentals, our breaths filled now
with sacred words, filtering the darkness out.
Even the statues wear masks.

If missals and hymnals have been put away,
sing a Psalm softly to mute COVID devil's blare.
Holy water fonts are dry so they do not become
petri dishes incubating deadly spores.

Don't fret that the sign of peace has been suspended.
Try a nod, a bow, a wink, a wave, a smile, an elbow
bump, or pressing your hands together in prayer
to signal that COVID's plots do not work here.

Ventilators

The Statue of Liberty said it best—
America is *yearning to breathe free*,
but COVID is poisoning the democracy of our air,
targeting our weakest citizens, their lungs burning
and shriveling, blown apart because of invisible
land mines the plague has planted in polluted yellow air.

But ventilators have become national heroes, pushing
clean air in with plenty of oxygen chasers, and then
pumping sick air out with its noxious aerosol particles.
Hooked up to tubes and wires, the COVID-stricken gasp
to avoid swelling and scarring, hoping to go home,
escaping the virus's deadly tricks.

II: COVID Children

Polio Kids, Chicago, 1952

I remember those stifling August nights
I was put to bed before

sunset when the temps were still stuck
in the humid 90s, and the ambulances

panicked like air raid sirens back and
forth from the tenements

across the L tracks to Cook County Hospital
waiting for another shivering child who

caught polio and was quarantined
in one of those thumping coffins

pushing and pulling their breath in
and out and sounding like my mother's

old Hotpoint washing machine
wheezing in our second floor flat.

Every morning I used to feel my chest
to make sure it had not turned to iron.

An epidemic of absences hit
the Chicago public schools that fall.

Polio kids could not get to class or
down the hall to the bathroom;

their bones and muscles turned to jelly;
they had to wear steel creases in their pants

and lead stirrups that clicked and clanked;
they needed four rubber tipped arms as well.

The city was infected with contagious despair;
mothers smothered their children in gauze

to protect them; sneezing became
an act of sabotage in the war against

this rogue disease that robbed so many children
of their goldenrod dreams.

Hospitals put tilted mirrors
at the head of their iron lungs

so the kids inside could see
who was crying the most.

Memories of Breathing

COVID Summer of 2020 stirs my memory of breathing.
My uncle died as the pulmotor rushed to him at the VFW dance hall
back in July 1950 in Chicago. He begged for oxygen, blood gurgling
from his lungs. Then on the hottest night in 1955, when the air
was so thick you needed a hammer to break and breathe it, my mother
allowed me to trek into Lake Michigan's dark, chilly waters, so biting
I trembled for air. Years later, I remember my frightened panting
at the neighborhood pool when a throaty bully shoved me off
the deep end and I learned that water has different rules
for breathing than air does. My nose and mouth felt like they were
rinsed out with *Clorox*. When my son was four, I took him to see
fireworks in Winnetka, the air saturated with sulfur; he wanted to jump
over a chain link fence to find out more about how fallen stars exhale.
When I came to Mississippi in 1974, I watched old women walk
under their umbrellas in the humid, pulsating August sun to ward off
glistening beads of sweat settling on their faces and necks. To avoid
being winded they had to catch their breath before it left them.
I do not want to die in the summer, my body soaked with second-hand
air, soggy. I have asked my embalmer to keep me over until
cooler days when the air is crisp, dancing with cinnamon
and cranberries, and then let me be buried with the last of the leaves and
the rest of my family who pass in my dreams as calm, solemn breezes.

School Days

"Dear old golden rule days
Reading, and writin', and rithmetic
Taught to the tune of the hickory stick."

1907

Schools are battlefields now, students hiding behind
masks as they stand glued six feet apart; their laughter,
songs, and sports curtailed. Each day they must
wipe down their desks and wash, wash
their hands to fight off Corona monsters who prowl
about the campus seeking to devour them.
And still the air is filled with sneezes and coughs
as killer germs sneak into books and onto paper;
libraries are shut down. And the war goes on as droplets
invade lockers, doorknobs, desks, and handrails.
Like snipers COVID wait for students and teachers
in auditoriums, labs, gyms, cafeterias, hallways, stairwells.

A Child Reads the Pandemic

The parks are empty. Even the clouds
have gone. My friends don't call me
anymore to come outside. There is no
outside anymore. Everyone wears
masks now, afraid of those droplets
falling on us. It's like the Blitzkrieg
has come to New Jersey.

The Corona witch has stolen my daydreams
and drowned me in her nightmares.
Sirens wake me with their death rattles.
The pandemic has devoured my future.
My school's draped in black crepe.
I've even forgotten which grade I'm in.

Grandma lives only two blocks away,
but she might as well be in Marchen.
I haven't hugged her for months.
If she died, we couldn't go to her funeral.
No one could. Even the undertakers
can't touch a body unless
it is covered with PPE.

I live now in the city of the dead.
I have read about Anubis in one of my books.
At dusk yesterday, I saw a jackal running
across our backyard.

Coronials, 2020

We're the children of the pandemic
conceived by parents in quarantine
who dared to touch one another
in a cramped, one bedroom flat—
Adam and Eve in a lockdowned Eden.

We're the offspring of their boredom.
No bars, no ballgames, no restaurants,
no gatherings at friends' houses, no jobs.

Some of us will be born this Christmas;
others will come in the spring of 2021. We will be
labeled the COVID Kids or the Quaranteens,
citizens of this new unchartered normal.

It looks like we may never be able to go to school,
play sports, work outside our homes,
see a movie, go to a dance, a disco,
or believe announcements from the CDC,
FDA, CIA, or Planned Parenthood.

A vaccine needle symbolizes our future.
Without that there's no way forward.
Still there's no way to postpone our entrance
into America. Our birth certificates
wear black borders.

COVID Ate My School Lunch

That voracious COVID monster
ate my lunch as well as my breakfast
and after school snack. When the panedmic closed
our schools, it also locked up the cafeterias
that fed me and more than 30 million students
who depended on them to be our kitchen.

The COVID-caused food gap is terrifying . We have
become shivering skeletons; voices and tears few hear.
With both my parents out of work, there is scarcely
any food at home except a loaf of green bread, a torn
box of stale cereal, a couple of cans of *Sunny
Delight*, and rarely a .99 cent McDonald's hamburger
split three ways. My brother jokes that we are getting
our nutrition now from the kitchen faucet. No wonder
there's a rumor that rickets will soon be spreading
all over the Bronx.

Grubhub or *Uber Eats* never deliver in my neighborhood.
We are waiting for someone to bring us a few loaves of bread
and maybe some fish.

COVID Child Abuse

It always happens late at night.
The walls can't hold any more tears.
They swell with insults, threats, screams.

Our father's voice lashes at us like a whip,
leaving welts on our memories.
We're trapped, under house arrest,

ankle-braceleted to his moods. We never
see teachers, friends, counselors.
The church steeple has gone silent.

We live inside a crisis. COVID has
electrocuted family care with high wire
stress. No jobs, no prospects. Our hearts

and stomachs are so hungry. We doubt we
will have a future. All the phone lines to the
domestic abuse number stay jammed.

III: Hunger and Discrimination

The Potato Famine, Ireland, 1845

It was the *Gort Mor*, the Great Hunger, the blight
that took a million souls off to eternity
and sent that number or more to America and beyond.

It snuck its way from Mexico and sucked the life
out of the potato crop. A working man ate his way through
12-14 pounds a day, skin and all, and with a little luck

a bit of bacon and butter. But the blight did away
with all that. We tried to dig up the tubbers
the fungus forgot, but there were not enough
to keep an old woman from her grave.

The Famine Queen and our London masters turned
their backs on our bloated bellies and unsalted tears,
salt being a luxury we could ill afford.

How COVID Starves America

COVID, you have taken the food from the mouths
of millions of Americans, quarantined
children's stomachs, and socially distanced them
from sitting down for three meals a day.

These Trick or Treaters had to learn
to make *Tootsie Rolls* last till Thanksgiving
so they could take the place of drumsticks.

The Salvation Army now uses oil drums
instead of red kettles to beg for the starving.
And its not just for the chronic poor
but those whose jobs you stole turning them
into the new mega class of beggars.

Wal-Mart is capitalizing on their tragedy by selling
laminated signs *Will Work for Food* so that
they can plead at night.

But thanks to you, COVID, there is no shortage of tears
to swallow; but there are not enough counselors
to store them in their offices. But God saves them in his bottle.

The Dark Side of the Economy

Loan sharks, slumlords, repo men, IRS leviers —
all look up to you, Queen Corona! Just see
the crowds that you stripped of everything. Houses
under water that will never float a loan again.
Bus drivers and sanitation crews all sitting idle.
Waiters without tables, their tablecloths sold
for shrouds. Small business signs disappearing —
also employees without jobs, paychecks, insurance,

futures. America is thinner and breadlines stretch longer.
Stimulus checks are a thin memory. The COVID poor dine
on tossed paper plates and drink from empty milk cartons,
and raid garbage can. *No fishing* signs are placed over
manhole covers. Kids fight pigeons for crumbs.

Nuestra Nueva Casa

Corona is a cruel landlord taking over people's bodies,
cancelling their lease on life and throwing them out

of their hovel apartments, more than 40 million
this year alone. How can they come up with

back rent when they have no jobs. Corona profiteers
hide their eyes and close their hearts and hands

as the least of these, many of them Latinx strangers
in an unfriendly land, become street people overnight.

It begins with a knock, a summons, and ends with a padlock.
All their belongings packed in few black plastic bags

for the trip to the street. But how can you put sheets
over the pavement or where can you hang clothes

or curtains. Will the US Post Office deliver
to an address that has no address?

Passers-by glibly say these immigrants should
be grateful that America has donated

fouled Corona air. They can't get that in such abundance
in their own countries. Some wait outside funeral parlors

for a vacancy, or sneak into a post office
to bring back heat in a blanket

for a child or wife too sick to walk.
The street becomes their hospital, too.

Ambulances rushing by provide the only
medical care they will see all night.

Other *desalojos* crowd into a friend's already
overflowing apt., setting up households in a hallway

or sharing a bedroom with four generations,
the best housing arrangement for Corona

to spread. Shelters are great welcoming centers, too,
for Corona-evicted tenants packed face to face, coughs

and sneezes in lieu of rent. Corona quips it never
evicts anyone. Everyone's lungs are welcome.

Blue Collaring During COVID

They are the first to be laid off,
and the last to be hired back.

And when they are, they can't work
from a comfortable laptop at home.

Their remote job site can be two or even three
hours away, and clocking in late because of

snow, accidents, no money for carfare, missed
buses result in a pink slip

aimed like a bullet at them
and their families. Their children

go hungry and have no one to watch them;
daycare has drained their parents' pockets.

Digital on their job means working
with enslaved fingers and hands,

serving food, cleaning rooms, changing
beds, watching someone else's children, driving

delivery trucks, and often being assaulted by unmasked
bosses and customers who cough and sneeze

on them. Too many of these workers are destined
to be among COVID's fatalities.

Corona, You Are A Racist

Corona, haven't black and brown souls
been through enough suffering and suffocation
in the year of trumped up hate? So many

voices ended by chokeholds or knees pressed on
windpipes, lives lynched away. *"I can't breathe,"*
"I can't breathe," our new national requiem.

Your tactics are similar to those of
Felon Sheriff Joe Arpaio's Arizona prison
where Latinos were fevered to death.

You are the Bull Connor of viruses,
clubbing your victims into arrest across
an Edmund Pettus Bridge of sepsis.

Bigoted as Gov. George Wallace, you stand outside
hospitals denying your victims entrance
to emergency rooms.

Though you do not have eyes, you have singled out
these souls of color to fulfill half your death quotas.
Who says black and brown lives do not matter.

IV: Naysayers

Pharaoh's Ten Plagues

Your Nile, a river of blood, water hemorrhaging fish,
an invasion of spadefoot toads, frogs, everywhere frogs,
in the fields, in courtyards, sliming your canopied houses green,
in your bedrooms, on your walls, through your windows, on everything
you touch. Hiccupped laughter mocks you Pharaoh, stinking Egypt
with a smell that reached your nose-holding gods. Then came the lice,
and the fleas, throughout your kingdom of sand; your queen wore them;
they brought itching so burning, so intense, so unrelenting
that every Egyptian was tattooed with scabs, then ready for the boils, those
pus-erupting miniature volcanoes that adorn the bodies of your subjects;
you wearing the most. Now watch for the squadron of flies, a curse
on your god of flies, as they, too, invade your weeping land, buzzing
infection and assurances of doom; watch your croplands, too, Pharaoh,
your trees, your livestock as a thorny pestilence of locusts sweeps over
your dominion, leaving Egypt weak, powerless, the fool of the myths
you have enshrined in your gods—aptly personified as asses, snakes,
dogs, flies, winged vultures—and in your pale heart. Fiery hail will
purify the corruption of slavery and idolatry that rule your kingdom.
Because your cankered mouth refused to let the Israelites go, darkness
descends, a deep Biblical darkness, and for three days your first borns
will be smothered. And still you did not let the Israelites go. And at last
the Red Sea opens your mouth and your drown.

COVID *Abattoir*

Upton Sinclair is roiling in his grave.
Things have not changed in Packingtowns
across America. COVID has made them worse.

The virus multiplies in these damp, cold, sun-
blocked meat processing plants where billions of droplets
settle to slay much longer. Gigantic fans spread
this foul air as the workers breathe in each other's
infected coughs and sneezes squeezed in
cramped spaces.

Packed shoulder-to-shoulder, workers butcher
in exhausting, nonstop 10–12-hour shifts, no plexiglass
or strip curtains between them. Processing lines
move at drag car race speeds, leaving workers more
vulnerable. It's a lung-breaking job. And sharing knives
and hammers, shaking hands with COVID co-worker.

Like the animals whom they skin and eviscerate,
these meat processors leave the plant at shift's end
with slaughtered lives, their lungs and hearts become offal.

It's a jungle in there.

"Screw COVID. I Went to Sturgis."

For ten days, in the midst of the pandemic,
half a million scarf-headed, unmasked bikers
invaded Sturgis, South Dakota (population 7,000),
vrooming, promenading, nightclubbing, leering over
bikini wrestling, screaming, vrooming their coughs
and sneezing. Social distance is a joke here.
What better sanitizer than a bottle of *Bud Light*?

Only the Cheyenne have stopped them from trespassing
on tribal lands. Still, the bikers throw out bravado lines
that sound like *Rolling Stones* lyrics. *"Live for the kicks."*
*"You'll never know the fun if you don't go." "If I die
from the virus, it was meant to be."* Like their MAGA Potus,
they prophesize that *"It is what it is"* and *"Sturgis
is the place to do it!"* Ecce angelus mortem.

Cruising up and down beer can paved streets on their Harleys,
Bobbers, Indians, Streetfighters, Triumphs, and Choppers,
they rival the fertility festivals of ancient, booze-soaked
Egypt, or the Dionysian gang bangs in sinking Rome
where drunken charioteers were followed by orgies
of naked women and parades paying homage
to a gigantic wooden phallus.

Sturgis has become America's hottest place to party.
But soon enough the bikers will fever their way back home
as they pass through Deadwood.

Hydroxychloroquine

What's a pandemic without a snake oil
salesman with his quick, quack cures—
magic bullets, fumigants, Chinese oil.
In 1347, a plucked live chicken or cut up
snake was rubbed on black buboes
to make them go away. They didn't.
Instead, 50 million souls perished.
Then nerve pills, colicky pellets, and quinine
laxatives were peddled as sure cures for
the Spanish Flu. The only thing sure was they didn't work.

2020. Enter Dr. Trump with his script,
prepared by slimy money Pharma lobbyists,
selling hydroxychloroquine (not to be confused
with hydrophobia) and explaining how this risky drug
(FDA revoked) got rid of COVID-19.
It also got rid of many who swallowed it.

Judging by its side effects—yellow eyes, anxiety,
dizziness, depression, jerky movements, coronary
irregularities, and hallucinations—Dr. Trump
should know the drug well, suffering as he does
from many of these symptoms.

Still he declares: *"It's our Constitutional right to try it."*

The Rallies

Overwhelming numbers of MAGA members crowd into
outdoor and indoor arenas, rally grounds, stadiums, airplane
hangers, and grandstands rivaling those at Zeppelinfeld.
They are outfitted in uniforms of conflict, blood red caps,
tattooed slogans, insignias of white power, white rule,
all oblivious to the virus lurking in their breath. They come
to see their superhero, watch his swag, listen for
his dog whistles, be hypnotized by his barbed rhetoric
as he propagandized the air recruiting droplets
from their boos and yells. Their voices march in tune
with his vendettas as he gleefully serves up scapegoats
for them to execute with their voices—*"Lock her up." "Take back
Pennsylvania." "Kung Flu." "Fight like hell."* He rouses them for war.
Little do they know or care that 10 percent of them
could be responsible for infecting the other 90 percent.
The more they shout their venom, the greater the risk.
His base followers eagerly bring two viruses home with them—
COVID-19 and "Make America Hate Again."

Dr. Fauci the Prophet

Dr. Fauci, prophet of the COVID plague,
was sent to preach caution and calm
in these times of fire, times of a ranting tyrant,
in a land cursed with countless miseries,
blasphemous acts of recklessness, and death.

A smiling Jeremiah, the five-foot, seven-inch Fauci
stood up to a blustering six-foot, three-inch Goliath
who keeps bragging that we're around
the corner with the plague. *"Open the country,"*
he roars. *"Forget about masks." "COVID is a hoax."*
But Dr. Fauci prophesizes that doing that will take us
on the wrong course.

Like Jeremiah, too, Fauci has been punished for speaking
the truth in this kingdom of fevers. He was thrown
into a befouling cistern, kept from public appearances,
silenced by the tyrant bearing the red mark of the beast
on his head and screaming, *"Fire Fauci. Fire Fauci."*
But Fauci's prescription has turned into a prophecy:
"The tyrant is the virus. Get rid of him and heal the country."

Masks No Longer Required, Right!

March 2, 2021

Unmask yourselves, Texans,
howled the governor. I am opening
the state 100 percent right now.

Breathe all over Texas, folks,
from the polluted air of Port Sulphur
to crowded tears in El Paso.

Lift your masks. Show your faces
at bars on Galveston Bay, restaurants
in Austin, churches everywhere.

No one will pester or penalize you
for not following a lame law
no longer needed.

We are not in the business
of telling people what they can
and cannot do anymore.

Forget Dr. Fauci claiming we opened up
too soon or Beto's accusation that
I issued a death warrant to Texans.

Only 200 people die a week in Texas
now from COVID. The pandemic is
behind us.

We are not the lone state starring
in pulling down mask regulations.
Kudos to my fellow governors in

Florida, Mississippi, and North Dakota
for joining us in riding herd over unfair
mask orders foolishly promising immunity.

The Vaccine — the Phases

Begin with monkeys and mice,
spirit totem animals, family protectors,
strength bearers, the first to enter the battlefield.

Next come a small group of healthy, nameless
heroes without fear of an early tombstone.
They are commandoes who under cover of
their flesh got an initial dose of COVID to see
if a trial vaccine might save us.

Then a profusion of subjects, a cross-
section of ages including seniors with grey
veins and wrists that tick like clocks
winding down, our most vulnerable, hoping
their immune systems will produce enough antibodies
to overcome the enemy, ghoulish COVID.

Over months, and more months, tests,
a triage of records, side effects, breakthroughs,
adjuvants and antigens, setbacks,
reviews, hard-eyed regulators' vetoes,
then more tests, pauses, obituaries, bodies
unrecognized for their martyrdom.
A cure now is within an arm's reach.

But still some don't believe in the pandemic
and wonder why a vaccine is even necessary.

V: COVID's Long Haul

On a Quarantined Ship, Cholera Outbreak, 1752

The gulls' cries go adrift; but we are locked
in iron waves, our ship has become a *lazaretto*,
one yellowed death following another.
No harbor will berth us. The shore threatens to fire
on us if we come closer than three leagues.

They think distance will protect them from us.
But what will protect us from them? We scrub
the decks, paraffin chipped planks, but even so
each day our hearts grow thinner,
our breath more matted,
our ribs poking through our flesh like bail wire.

Our hammocks have become swinging tombs.
The mocking sun only makes the fever hotter,
our mouths and throats thirst, and blood-sprayed coughs
precede the dreaded rattle; and another life is lowered into
the sea's black void as whales intone high-pitched dirges.

At night we light our cholera lanterns and pray,
remembering that angels brought Christ
food after 40 days in the desert. But we fear
that for many this quarantine will last a lifetime,
maybe longer.

Variola's Boasts

I gave mummies that rash that glowed
through the millennia. I also wiped out
Columbus' Indians. I blinded children
and flooded cities with rivers of vomit.

I spring from rats, voles, cows, and cats
and knocked down peasants and courtiers
with tar-hot fevers sending them
under the earth to decay.

I am the *Speckled Monster* who left pus-filled
red buttons on faces, genitals, and limbs,
and then turned them into abscesses and scabs
letting them marinade into charred skin.

I loved turning my victims' bodies
into craters. My legacy — "A pox on you."

Voting Ghosts

The ghosts of Summer 2020 will not rustle away
with fall's panicky breath. More than
the population of Amarillo, Des Moines,
Montgomery, Reno, or San Bernardino,
they cry out for their pre-COVID bodies,

clamoring to make their mark on a ballot
or stand in long lines to ensure their names are not erased at the polls.
They vow to hold up their registration cards
and wear their photographs while chanting the 14th Amendment.

They have been victims of someone else's numbers
and want to change, if only they could, a future
that excluded them. They are ready to riot for righteousness.
What does it matter if they wear dust in their hair or speak
in halting syllables, these more than three hundred thousand dead
in this grave new world.

COVID Autumn, 2020

COVID autumn and the winds are whipping up
the stale air of summer, along with germs
that have already killed more than 300,000 souls
in America. Do you catch plague faster

when the weather cools? So many fallen
souls like crushed pieces of the sky cry out
for tenderness as their blue bodies are hauled
off to a COVID morgue.

No wonder we have worn masks all year long.
Halloween's not restricted to just a few hours.
It's been here all fall as boney Death goes door
to door trying to trick us to let our masks down.

And then comes Thanksgiving with no family
gatherings, afraid that they will bring COVID inside.
Black Friday's been extended through the winter,
though shopping for bargains this year could be deadly.

Pandemic Fatigue

Each day unremembers the one before.
Nothing changes but the numbers.
Thank God—I am not yet one of them.
I repeat the same version of myself.

Dust gathers hourly on these pictures
that once brought us yesterday's love.
Anger in the streets replays
what I feel inside, kept hidden
in the exhaustion of monotony.

Our house has become a metronome
of mood swings morphing into
each other, a junkyard of dreams.
The only thing that keeps growing is rust.

COVID Brain Fog

Ever since COVID invaded me,
it has never left my thoughts.

My brain has slowed down, exhausted,
unable to escape the quicksand
my words have wandered into

but never out of. I couldn't pull
them out to carry on a conversation,
let alone ask for help.

People talking sound like
mumbling foghorns; I get dizzy
listening to them.

My eyes cry rain,
and I forget what air
tasted like.

Wailing ghosts mist
my windows; and the stars
wear masks; the sky

is colorless; vague winds
wrap me into insomnia.
I stay up to go to my own funeral.

Long Haulers

COVID visited us but never left.
The moderate bout of 14 days has turned
into more than 100 days with 100 different symptoms,
so many that with COVID brain fog we cannot recall them all
except for persistent coughs, coughs that throw our bodies
into spasms triggering more coughs.

And then there's the draining fatigue; we cannot even shut off
a faucet, get the mail, or work more than half an hour
each day. Our legs fold under us like a card table
and we collapse. On so many days we cannot
get out of bed. But sleep is never restful; high fevers
make us feel as if the house is on fire

and we will go up in flames with it.
Our lungs, heart, kidneys, and guts have threatened
to abandon us; they cannot endure the pain
or the uncertainty of what COVID is doing to us.
Our skin hurts; our bodies ache as if we were in a pillory.
Our calendars read like a medical record—so many visits
to the ER, hospitalizations, trips to specialists, trips for
X-rays, MRIs, injections, breathing treatments.

COVID plays no favorites; it has invaded children,
young adults, the middle aged, and a country of seniors,
but it never ends with better health. We fear
that COVID will be with us till death do us part.

COVID's Strains

Across countries and continents they spread
faster than flu or HIV. Like chameleons
they change their shape and their scowls.

They are trying to sneak in without
a passport or even a photo i.d.
Border patrols cannot catch what
they cannot see or interrogate a renegade
that refuses to have a voice.
They replicate themselves in a nanosecond.

They come to infiltrate our sinuses,
brain synapses, joints, and our mobility.
And they have vowed to invade
our domestic lungs.

True, some will not stick around for a long time,
but those that do have sworn to take down
anyone whose body has already paid tribute
to death master COVID. These strains pose a double
jeopardy for over 500,000 in America alone.

The Dark Winter, 2020–2021

COVID has brought us into this dark season
of unhope, seeping into us like the damp.
Nature offers no soft snowflake manger.
Breathing doesn't seem right. The air smells
like rancid holly and feels like we're breathing
piercing pines. Trees have morphed into
sullen pallbearers draping the sky with black sap.
The hollow voice of the wind howls endless obituaries.

Holiday voices toll like a sextant's bell.
Ghostly gray faces sit across crowded
family tables but do not see their COVID guests
gleefully spreading deadly cheer, droplets
infecting those gathered to hug, kiss, shake
hands, laugh, and share stories and soon ICU beds,
COVID's ultimate indoor holiday celebrations.

Sheltering

"I'll never let another patient of mine pass
without being there for him or her."

— Critical care nurse, St. Vincent's,
Billings, Montana, November 2020

These are the saints of the Corona scourge:
doctors, nurses, respiratory therapists, EMTs,
all who shelter their patients from low oxygen,
rales and rattles, life's final exhaling.

Pieta-like, they embrace the poor
and rejected, those hidden behind blood-
splotched curtains, quarantined from family.
They defy the safe limits of touch

to hold hands with the dying and give them
the consolation of togetherness. They break
words with them for a last communion and bring Gilead
to Brooklyn, Siloam to Billings. They try to slow
the tolling, the incessant tolling of lives lost.

Their rewards are scored in rousing orchestras
of applause, and in flutes, trumpets, and hurrahs hurled
from city balconies, seventy times seven feet above
the streets, as these saints annoint the dying with tears.

A Sailor Dies in the ICU

The nights are endless; no windows
not even a door. Only curtains—
a sail maker's tarp quizzing mates
whether life or death is on

the other side. He feels like a diver;
tubes and hoses, snorkels pumping
air into his windless lungs billowing up
only to sink again.

He dreams he is going down to the Gulf
this afternoon as he did five decades
ago to fish in the sun-stroked air;
he can feel the sand in his throat—

so hard to sing to the mermaids.
The currents keep shifting, moving
the shore closer or farther away depending
on how high their dirges moan.

Everything is a blur; he must have left
his eyes at home or in the ER;
he does not need them. His memory
helps him read headlines published

a lifetime ago about ships foundering.
But he wonders why everyone around
him wears a lifejacket. Are they afraid
of drowning in the foggy sea air.

Seven bells sound. The air drowns his voice.

Saying Goodbye

You are a cruel thief, COVID. You stole
our father away and then stripped him
of his dignity and our care in his fatal hours.
We could not visit him, not even peek
through the ICU glass windows.

Through FaceTime, though, we saw
he was living in a different body, exiled
to a world of whirls and a maze of IVs;
his bludgeoned arms shriveled and shackled;
his swollen face a beehive strapped
under an iron oxygen mask.

We tried to call him but he could not hear us.
An ocean churned in his cubicle; his voice became
ventilator hums, suction tube gurgles, rattles,
crash cart bangs, and IV beeps, a Braille of sounds
we could not read.

No wake, no funeral. COVID, you took even these.
All we were left with was a family of tears,
and a crumpled pall of *Kleenex*.

Calls from the Hospital

The cell phone was our waiting room.

Our ears cried every time
it rang.

First came a light, followed
by the ring

and a staccato voice—
our fright hesitated to

catch up with the pauses,
then the repetition of *ums*

and a flood of polysyllabic words.
We braced ourselves

against a calendar,
tears holding us there like cement.

Stable until midnight,

then, then, then
the worst word

in the medicine of hope,
endlessly losing

our mother, despite
trying to hold on to her.

fever yet another terror word—
we could feel our mother's temp

rising through the voice
that was charting it.

No more reports the rest of the night
unless . . .

 another lethal word
that projects nightmares

of her becoming a skeleton
shrouded in tubes.

And then the last call
from the hospital,

putting us on hold,
waiting, waiting until

finally connecting us
to the morgue.

VI: Spangled Banners
for the COVID Dead

A Doughboy Reflects on the Spanish Influenza, 1918

It killed more of us than the Kaiser's poisoned gas,
scorching our lungs, drowning us in our own spittle.
The stronger our bodies, the more fluids we had,
the faster the Spanish Lady caught us.

The camps were induction centers for pestilence.
Barracks, chow lines, showers, privies —
all saturated with bombs exploding inside us.
Blue and purple-lit faces shouted at us in our dreams.

One doctor watched two brothers die 30 minutes
apart as they stretched out to hold each other's hand.
Danger telegrams reached families too late;
too many of us died before we ever went over there.

If we did make it, the vile trench fever dug deep
deep into our lungs. Trenches stretched over 500 miles,
averaging more than 25 bodies per mile.
The sky above Ardennes couldn't wake dead stars.

The number of soldiers needed for battle was cut
in half as men were assigned to care for the sick.
The Hun suffered, too, as the plague criss-
crossed battlefields as easily as a Zeppelin.

At last, we buried many of the infectious dead
in the Alaska permafrost. No white crosses;
only snow drifts to blanket the fallen.

18-Wheel Mausoleums

A shift has almost ended

but nothing can be done to add a cubit to the life
of these Corona souls.

They lacked the strength to toil
and spin another hour on a ventilator.

Doctors' and nurses' tears burn right through
their N-95s.

Sorrowing is limited to wherever two or three gather,
though the coroner prefers a gathering of one.

The hospital morgue overflows with bodies
in basement crypts; they also pile up

in hallways, in corners, on gurneys waiting
in the driveway, and on the mourning streets.

Refrigerated 18-wheel mausoleums are now parked
just beyond the precincts of pain.

Churches send myrrh-scented body bags
so these souls will have wedding garments

to wear on their journey to the everlasting.
Each grips a passport to immunity.

The Long Line of COVID Dead

COVID corpses come before me
heroes of a war fought between
coughs and freezing fevers,
assaults on their drowned lungs.
May they wear stars and stripes forever.

These brave dead come, and they come,
like waves of grain, our new heroes
in six point *New York Times* type.
We need magnifying glasses to salute them.
Let their spangled banners wave.

But where are the proclamations, declarations,
national obsequies for these COVID-struck citizens,
a national treasure heaved into morbidity reports.
These dead shall not have died in vain.

How many names, faces, lives forgone,
impaled in dust, not in patriotic ink
where they should have spent their eternity.
Hail to them from sea to shining sea.

It is their right and our duty to honor them,
these lost battalions of slain COVID prisoners of war,
but none flown to Dover AFB, escorted by an honor guard
with braided shoulders and cadenced steps,
wheeling their brass-handled glistening coffins.
We owe tributes to these fallen under God.

A Country of Corpses

We may never know the numbers for sure.
Some died in their homes, their sofas makeshift caskets.
Some authorities say victims died of the flu or emphysema.
Some agencies list only deaths on hospital beds,
ignoring other places COVID raided. Elsewhere
death certificates are delayed and weekend mortalities
excluded. The homeless are quietly cremated.

Who infects who is a terrifying mystery.
You cannot count on accurate numbers.
Government websites boast that
they track and compare COVID deaths
by state, age, race, and a long obituary
of other tokens, but again how many souls
have been left out.

And some countries mask the real numbers
to escape censure and gain applause for handling
the pandemic better with fewer casualties.

And then some claim the pandemic is a hoax,
even as the lists of the dead get longer and longer.

They Have All Gone
into the World of Light*

A new president, a *novus ordo seclorum*,
a new prayer for all those COVID dead
who have gone into the world of light.

Four hundred candles along the reflecting pool
between Washington and Lincoln's watch,
each candle becoming a light for every 1,000 dead

who have perished. *To heal we must remember.*
And so there stand the Bidens and the Harrises,
their silence a eulogy for victims and their families.

Each loss an exceptional soul honored
in countless hearts, memories, and
in Arlingtons all across America.

Let their candles be anthems of light.

*These words come from a poem by 17th-century poet
  Henry Vaughan.*

VII: Hope and Beyond

The Vaccines — at Last

In the dark winter of our suffering
came vaccines from the grail
of science, holy chrism in a vial
to fell this blasphemous COVID-19.

Decades of research packed into seven months
of testing and more testing. But now they are ready.
Nameless COVID scientists join the noble order
of medical heroes like Pasteur, Ehrlich, Salk, and Snow
in bestowing the blessing of protection on us.

Still, thousands cry, *Too late, too late,*
their graves and ashes roiling in anguish,
wishing the vaccines had come sooner.
Our grief is the repayment of their love.

Thanks be that now hope extends to their loved ones
who will reach sanctuary just by rolling up
their sleeves and receiving a 10 second-injection
in exchange, we pray, for a lifetime of surety.

COVID, where is your sting now.

The COVID Relief Bill, March 2021

Manna in the form of relief checks
now flows into our dried up savings
accounts. Food at last in this COVID
drought. *Ramen Noodles* marinated
in water no longer our national diet.
We can eat meat, pay rent, stop chopping
dad's blood pressure meds into fours.
He no longer has to wipe the clots off
his brow and legs. We can afford aspirin.
Half of America's children can at last come
out of poverty and back to school. Their IQs
and moods will inevitably go up. They can
now cover their bones with food-fed flesh.
Gone are Trump's mandates for enforced starvation.
Working for him never made us free.
Thank you, Joe, for starving COVID and not us.

Author's Biography

Philip C. Kolin is the Distinguished Professor of English (Emeritus) and Editor Emeritus of the *Southern Quarterly* at the University of Southern Mississippi. He has published more than 40 books on Shakespeare, Tennessee Williams, and contemporary African American women playwrights and twelve collections of poetry. Among these are *Emmett Till in Different States* (Third World Press, 2015), *Reaching Forever* (Poiema Series, Cascade Books, 2019), *Delta Tears* (Main Street Rag, 2021), and *Wholly God's* (Wind and Water Press, 2021). The 12th edition of his business and technical writing textbook *Successful Writing at Work* will be published by Cengage Learning in 2022. Kolin has also coedited three eco-poetry anthologies on Katrina, the Mississippi River, and the moon. He is now at work on a memoir tentatively entitled *Always Pilsen: Growing Up on Chicago's Near West Side.*

www.ingramcontent.com/pod-product-compliance
Lightning Source LLC
LaVergne TN
LVHW051705080426
835511LV00017B/2746